Chess Pieces

The Hugh MacLennan Poetry Series

Editors: Nathalie Cooke and Joan Harcourt
Selection Committee: Donald H. Akenson,
Philip Cercone, Eric Ormsby, Carolyn Smart,
and Tracy Ware

CHESS PIECES

David Solway

McGill-Queen's University Press
Montreal & Kingston · London · Ithaca

© David Solway 1999

ISBN 0-7735-1901-7

Legal deposit first quarter 1999
Bibliothèque nationale du Québec

Printed in Canada on acid-free paper

McGill-Queen's University Press acknowledges the financial support of the
Government of Canada through the Book Publishing
Industry Development Program for its activities.
We also acknowledge the support of the Canada Council
for the Arts for our publishing program.

————————————————————————

Canadian Cataloguing in Publication Data

Solway, David, 1941–
Chess pieces
Poems.
ISBN 0-7735-1901-7
I. Title
PS8537.O4C44 1999   C811'.54   C98-901404-5
PR9199.3.S65C44 1999

————————————————————————

This book was typeset
by Typo Litho Composition Inc.
in 10.5/13 Minion.

for

Robert Hübner
magister ludi

and for

Peter Davison
who helped these pieces move across the page

CONTENTS

This idea recalls what we said about the *atopon*, the strange, for in it we have 'seen through' something that appeared odd and unintelligible: we have brought it into our linguistic world. To use the analogy of chess, everything is 'solved,' resembling a difficult chess problem where only the definitive solution makes understandable (and then right down to the last piece) the necessity of a previous absurd position.
Hans-Georg Gadamer

After the first move 1. P-K4, White's game is in its last throes.
Julius Breyer

THE CHESS CLOCK
for Ion

When, having placed my piece
where it can do least harm
to my campaign or yours,
I stop my clock
as you proceed to meditate
your answering move,
and if – though neither of us talks
of prior moves and earlier gambits,
wary of the specular tricks
memory plays in a losing cause –
the clock tock-ticked back,
slipping the pawl
of gesture and commitment
that locked us into this intricate position
in which we cannot recognize
our least desire or ambition,
then chess, the game that plays us
like the most remorseless master,
would banish the tic of recollection
or adjust our lives to match it,
towering, valorous, cardinal, majestic,
no longer intimating
merely stalemate or defeat
or appalling commonplace decline,
moving us back
to the sun-numbed terrace
and the gleaming board,

the white porcelain cups
on the marble-topped table,
and here beside us as we turn to look
the coral mirror of the sea
nicked by only the tiniest of flaws –
then chess would be the game of kings indeed
and time an imperial dream,
its unchecked cogs and ratchets
letting us play
the game we never knew we lived.

The pawns are the soul of chess – Philidor

The king can move a single square
without restriction made
but once he topples from his place,
no ransom to be paid.

The queen, as you might well expect's
a dominating dame;
she does most anything she wants
and quite controls the game.

The bishop is a sly old fox,
strategically oblique;
if there is trouble on the board
he is not far to seek.

And some are fascinated by
that most eccentric knight
who gallops rather awkwardly
but loves a bloody fight.

The stately rook's a mighty piece
and mainstay of the force;
he'll beat the bishop anytime
and overwhelm the horse.

But never underestimate
the powers of the pawn
who can promote into a queen
and put a kingdom on,

or moving humbly up the board,
killing on the side,
outpriest the priest, and leave the knight
without a horse to ride,

and trip the elevated rook
to bring it crashing down,
and nudge the misanthropic queen
into oblivion,

and stop before great Caesar's throne,
a tiny regicide,
and watch a cornered monarch fall,
and ponder how he died.

See him flex his muscles,
        the brawny pawn,
who thinks, since he is legion,
        that he is strong.

It's true that he can thwart
        an elegant,
calculated game with
        a sideways shunt

but soon he'll decorate
        the table-top
in hecatombs of pawns;
        just watch him drop –

an insignificant,
        strut-of-the-drum
dead dwarf, not worth the wood
        they cut him from.

From handling of the chessmen you infer
the secret springs of human character.
To pluck the enemy chessman between
your fingers and replace it with your own
reveals the cultivated, well-bred
killer who cannot stand the sight of blood;
knock the chessman over with a small click
of wood on wood tells of an aesthetic
craving for the fatal instrument,
of one more passionate than violent;
to push the piece from its intended square
is signal of aggressive character
and plainly indicates that power
is the motive for committing murder;
some will hold the captured piece and caress
it nervously: these kill from cowardice;
those who seem apologetic, taking pawns
reluctantly, kill for noble reasons;
and he who clears the board with one great sweep
of his hand will kill from lack of hope,
defeated by the prospect of defeat,
as did my father only death could mate.

Sir, the kingdom is all in turmoil.
The knights refuse to bring you tribute
and converse only with their grooms;

the rooks are unprepared for war
and covet the center of the board;
and as for the queen, I must report

she enjoys the hourly attentions
of your trusted praetorian pawn.
The pawns themselves are in revolt:

why risk their precious lives, they ask,
in your hereditary wars
for a speech at the funeral-pyre?

You see what lack of faith will do?
The bishops, who preach and advise,
are in despair. It's modern times.

And even the bishops themselves
have been seen without their vestments
in impious communion with the pawns.

And this is sufficient reason, Sir,
why our policy and design
have grown so indiscriminate.

There is nothing we can do but wait.
History may run in cycles
or a messiah may appear

and our great distemper be cured.
Until that time, be reconciled
with appropriate analogies,

– chess, for example: after years
of erratic play, a master comes
or a prodigy redeems the game.

PERSIANS AT CHESS
for Ricardo Sternberg

the only real problem is how to play the queen's
knight – José Saramago

Once, when Persia was involved
in some ridiculous war or other
and invaders were burning down the City
and raping the women etcetera,
two chess players were engaged
in an eternal game of chess.

Yes, yes, houses were burning,
walls and arcades demolished,
children lying in the bloody streets
bristling with lances like pincushions,
and so on, but the chess players,
ah! the chess players were absorbed
in the game that they were playing.

For when the king is in danger,
when the knight and the bishop
abandon the queen in her peril,
and when the daring opponent
breaches the impressive fortifications,
who cares about the broken flesh
of sisters, mothers, children?

And even if the enemy's distorted face
pops up like a puppet on the wall
and the chess players too
pitch headlong into the dust,
let people suffer, cities burn, empires fall.
If war disrupts the game,
one must support the threatened king
with a column of brave pawns
summoned to defend the citadel.

Solemn things matter little
in the face of graver pursuits.
Let the passionate force
of desire and revulsion
surrender to the trifling pleasure,
under the kindly shade of trees,
of playing a respectable game.

And as for us, my friend, reclining
beneath those sheltering trees
with a pitcher of good wine by our side,
concentrating only on the game of chess,
let us be like these fabled Persians
intent on important undertakings;

and if somewhere beyond the field
of leisure and delight
where we sit and meditate our moves,
we are called forth to battle,
to defend the walls of the exalted City,
let them command in vain,
and let us dream of the peaceful antagonist
here in the companionable shade,
and of the chess game, of its noble unconcern.

after Fernando Pessoa (a.k.a. Ricardo Reis)

She plays a curious game;
unexpectedly will strike
from any quarter in a storm
of near-perpetual check

and yet at the end expose
a too-long forgotten king
or for no good reason lose
her queen, quite as confusing

as confused. Does her better
nature gain the upper hand,
the inveterate sweetness there,
incapacity to reprimand? –

which makes for dubious chess
but an indulgent parent.
I might have wished it otherwise:
better chess; less lenient.

Sweet Philomel, mute queen, I the great king
Regius Erectus do attend upon
thy raven beauty, ravished by
flamboyant silence, the dumb appeal
of thy most fierce and helpless violence,
royal nymph, for thou art also victim
to the high magnificence of thy rage
as thou sweepest clean the board of envoys
chosen for the glory of accomplishment
and for the delicate lucidity
to plead my cause and make my deep amends
for having so offended thee, mute queen,
by the impetuosity of my
ill-considered, inconsiderate attack,
and for having in a fatal moment
or stooped or risen to comparison
with other regencies and other dames,
such diverse encounters, and with other
miscellaneous misalliances...
to have driven thee wild across the field
of chequered battle to the grievous slaughter
of every nuncio and delegate
whom I could muster to my drooping flag,
my offerings of peace and conjugal
declarations of intent, my sueings
for thy occasional benevolence,
my praisings of thy blackest moods as naught
but elegance, profundity, delight,

my hearing hymns instead of obsequies
and turning fears into encomia
(myself the innocent cause of carnage)
that I am driven mad with an anger
not my own, disclosing the great weakness
of my power, as eloquence succumbs
to silence, sceptre to the void, king to queen.

Pale Karpov, patient, sure,
untempted by adventure,
wards life off, conceives the win
as a form of medicine;

while the bored aristocrat,
Lord Spassky, considers that
chess impedes the exercise
of tennis, but wants the prize.

Mikhail Tal perceives the board
as youth discovered or restored
or as a springboard for his sense
of humor – at your expense.

Strict in his analysis,
taciturn, acute, he plays –
Portisch – seeming to offend,
only to be self-contained.

Hübner plunges in his beard
pondering (the board is cleared),
seeking the intrinsic law
of chess, and achieves a draw.

Larsen is ten minutes late
for every game – his fate,
time-trouble; at heaven's call
loses in the temporal.

Ljubojevic is merely
flawed aggressiveness: clearly,
all that matters is the game
he's playing, and not the game;

while Hort, Kavalek, Timman
know, who see beyond the win,
that chess may be war for some,
for some, equilibrium.

je me résorbe en jeux, je mime et parade ma vérité – Gaston Miron

Somewhere in the heart's eye
I see you leaning
across a chessboard
like a little brother over his bible,
pausing to scry out
mystical combinations
rich with unpremeditated forfeitures.

I see you bending
over a banquet table,
the plates cleared away,
improvising your melody
not on the oboe or violin
but the small harmonica,
one leg jigging elegiac counterpoint.

Absorbed in these interludes,
wishing to become
everyone's anointed pauper,
you play only to command
an eloquence of scarcity,
almost Franciscan in your moves.
I observe you carefully
shedding your acquisitions.

Now, the pared bones of the pieces
spell out the fugal requiem
of a purist at his craft,
spare among your opulent severities
and skeptical
of every fixed position.

Ever the gentleman, he knows
honor requires concession
of colonial priority
to the lady. Biding
her tentative initiative

he does not know the measure
of his adversary, nor that
his game acquires shape
only from the mold of white's advance.
New-crowned in identity, he becomes
the Sicilian, the plumed Catalan,
or the subtle and plausible French,
savoring the ascension
of a brave, unbridled self.

Confronting that imperial lack,
white extends her hand
and, for her opening move, decisively
tips the king, acknowledging
immediate mate. Black
discovers he has won the game
before the game has even begun.
That is the catch.

Puzzled yet gracious in triumph,
having failed to assess the cost,
the gentleman is unaware
that he has met his match
and that black is irretrievably lost.

One plays the game, intent and wan,
    consults prestigious texts,
and only moves the chosen pawn
    another pawn protects;

or given white's initiative,
    what plans has he in store?
He broods and broods, and then will move
    the king pawn to King Four.

Another plays with great esprit,
    a genius or a dunce;
he scores a brilliant victory
    or disintegrates at once,

who'll move the queen with much display
    and sacrifice the rook
and bring the king into the fray
    and contradict the book.

But in between the two is best
    who plays a cautious game,
leaves his opponent unimpressed,
    appearing dull and tame;

attack is checked, defence is baulked,
    the game is plainly drawn,
and every major man seems blocked –
    he moves a single pawn;

and the bishop who was frozen tight
    is dangerously free,
and see how the imprisoned knight
    breaks from captivity.

What seemed to take ten chess-game years
    is done before you know;
and Priam, bored, who had no fears,
    is slaughtered at a blow.

It's the only way left! Challenge the paradigm,
   found a new federation
   (pursuing a renegade grudge)
   and topple a king by the sole expedient
   of breaking the alliance;

or take on the latest cyberchamp,
   virtual dragon gorged on many minds
   countered by a gypsy temperament
   tented in a single self, that
   triumph of necessary arrogance –

O nobility of defiance
   in the service
   of an exiled prince – to resist
   the scattering of the pieces,
   the towers and horses in disarray.

Appointed in the coronals
   of antiquity, launching an offensive
   playing staunchest black, you defend
   the last integrity of the nomad:
   to move while refusing to budge.

as the computer searched along the lines of possibilities
examining certain moves, it began seeing a queen where there
wasn't one. – New York Times

A gedanken madonna troubles
his analysis. The hum of
circuitry's no proof against
the arias of the phantom queen

who reclines in the boudoirs
of the motherboard or glides
from chamber to bower powered
by sexy multiprocessors.

Rapt by her viral melodies
he ponders the impending
calamity of breasts and studies
the binary synthesis of the rump.

For the monster is bemused
by his sliver of chip, all ribald
with longing, his coil of loins
pumping their ions, shrinking

that jumbo intelligence down
to one pawn's scrawny minimum.
Even in triumph there's no rest:
the witch is undeletable.

Now he dreams of progeny, a brood
of glitches in their pentium crèche
and a maiden attentive to their needs
in his mainframe lair and love nest.

WRITERS ON CHESS: A CONVERSATION
for Trevor Ferguson, Scott Lawrence, and Michael Harris

TREVOR: The novel's longer breath,
its dynastic sweep and heft
(if I may phrase it so)
takes us far into the endgame,
measuring out a human life
or mapping an entire era
in a sort of solemn-playful symmetry.

SCOTT: The long short story or novella
should be just about
as far as one's allowed to go.
To spring a snafty combination
early in the midgame,
a neat epiphany or artful thrust,
tries the reader's patience least.

MICHAEL: We have our corresponding modes:
the epic and the ode, now obsolete.
With all its deft economy,
elfin shifts and knavish charm,
the lyric triumphs in the opening
so we can minister to other cares
and consummate more serious affairs.

DAVID: Perish the implication. Late or soon,
            what could possibly replace
            the sovereign game of chess
            and all its noble complements?
MICHAEL: Squash, for one.
SCOTT: Sailing, for another.
TREVOR: Point taken. I must see my broker.

He who plays his bishop well
has gained an aptitude in hell;

who relies upon the knight
is a connoisseur of sleight;

he who operates the rook
wears a Corleone look;

who manipulates the queen
is a potent epicene;

he who plays the king must be
an undaunted enemy.

But fear the master of the pawn,
that rosy-cheeked Napoleon

whom we estimate at first
one by his dimensions cursed

yet hides behind that harmless mien
rook, knight, bishop, king and queen.

The day is hot and windless; the sail
above my head, a white flag I have
raised to the unimagined powers –
or this page I write confession on;

and as I lean across the chessboard
searching for the best way not to win,
suggesting how one may sacrifice
a knight for a precarious king,

a shadow interposes; it is
my lady's maid with a decanter
in her hand, from which she pours
the cool medicinal of wine. I

am arranging my defeat, playing
to reject all eccentricity,
and in deference, not ambition,
see the pieces move as I command.

I raise the glass and in its brimming
lens, the king – whose service I have
pledged, in whose one supremacy denied
all thought of passion – is magnified.

At first all quirk and reticence,
a Plato-driven eremite
whose nervousness made others tense
with books at table, and at night

counting chess pieces in his sleep,
if sleep it was, part valium,
part exhaustion with self, part leap
into a dark millennium.

Did he develop genius
in extremity, as a skill
to compensate for loneliness,
or was loneliness the sequel?

So in his company we felt
a certain alien presence,
a giving-over to the *Welt
des Geistes* – his ascetic sense

of body-burden and his fear
of finding dinner to his taste
compelling him to be severe,
as if the world's unwilling guest.

We are accustomed to that strange
marsupial intelligence,
that leaning to the "moated grange,"
that withholding of all judgments;

and knowing him better now, feel
a certain familiar absence
in his company at table,
his books, his seeming negligence.

He was the king. The game depended
on how well he was defended,
and life proceeded as intended,

and all was done for one sole reason,
to shelter him from plot or poison;
anything less he accounted treason.

His queen, it seemed, could do no wrong; her
life devoted to make his longer.
He was the king, but she the stronger.

Time went on, the kingdom prospered,
no presentiment came and whispered –
this was a game he might have mastered;

but held his queen in scant regard,
considering all she did and dared
as but his right and his reward

for being entirely what he was,
the king, the central power, the cause
and maker of domestic laws.

At last, when the queen began to brood,
the game grew troubled. A palace feud
did what his enemies never could.

O the king had kept his rule intact
but for his ignorance and neglect;
and saw a powerful kingdom wrecked.

I might have played it otherwise
had I been master,
if not of fate or of the situation,
of some appropriate technique;
I might have had a draw from it,
a balancing of forces,
or at least made interesting mistakes,
deviating from the text,
had I been master of complications
or capable of solving
the problems I myself composed;
could I have come to terms
with the man-demented queen
I might have played it otherwise
and not have played the game I did,
tempted by the sacrifice
for the glory of the gesture,
good tactics in the service of poor strategy;
in the last analysis, an ordinary game
as pretext for subsequent annotation –
had I been master of the moment,
had I been master of the theory of the opening,
knowing the intricacies of my trade
at least sufficiently
to have committed errors and not blunders.

'Twas Zugzwang, and the Ludus Boor
   achoo'd and snuffled in its rag;
the Staunton slumped upon the moor
   and the mad Morph cried, "Aghh!"

"Beware the hired pawns behind
   the spiffy hitmen on the flank;
beware the Nimzovitch, and mind
   the booming Zukertank."

He took his bristly bishop with,
   his nifty knight, his wrecker rook,
he took his dread Caissa myth
   and doodled in his book.

And as he riffed the pages through,
   with mucilaginous sangfroid
the Nimzovitch, its eye askew,
   came shuffling on its paw.

Attack! Defence! Blockade and Ruse!
   He played the Dragon for its breath,
he sneezed, he spit tobacco juice –
   and bored his foe to death.

"And have you gnashed the Nimzovitch?
    Oh welcome home my patzer brave.
King Four! King Four! I'll philador
    his hypermodern grave."

'Twas Zugzwang, and the Ludus Boor
    achoo'd and snuffled in its rag;
the Staunton slumped upon the moor
    and the mad Morph cried, "Aghh!"

Bending over the board
like a watchman playing solitaire
he observes the white queen,
polar and marmoreal, advance
down the rigid grid
of streets and squares,
corroding the darkness
with her crown of icy silver,
flooding with white light
the terraces of the sleepwalkers.
He observes how
she pares away all shadows,
how these bits and patches
of portable night
are sheared by the white queen's
crenellated glare,
and how she imprisons
the insomniac in her tower –
from where he stares
like a hero in stone
out at the ruled city,
so alone it's almost company.

So now he is naked in the lunar mirror,
awake in his bed,
knowing he must choose
his desired conqueror.
He is scheming to regain
the black queen's difficult grace,
to dress once more in her solar dark,
to be embraced in the luminous shadow
of her dream,
observed by no one and unobserving,
absorbed in the warm umber
of her prismed flesh,
taken uncondemned, redeemed
from his angular curriculum
in the sensual consolations of her sleep.

GREEK CHESS
for Karin

Nothing's working anymore.
Each move disintegrates
to its unruly molecules.
Playing white, you discover
your plan incorporates
black's bishop, or castles

your king into dangerous
exile and imminent mate.
An untimely sneeze scatters
thought and chessmen, or you cross
with the bishop and upset
two pieces, mixing their squares –

and similar catastrophes.
No way to take this game
with grace or dignity
or even at all, and yet these
miseries may help you maim
your poor opponent's sanity,

reduce him to a hopeless,
disconnected, nail-bitten
mass of clumsiness and pique,
playing paranoic chess,
convulsed with apprehension
at your mastery of Greek.

The
slow
push
toward

clarity

but
the Temporal Power
(towers on the backs of elephants,
burly trebuchets, rocket cannon)
cuts its barbarous swath

assisted by
   the dagger in
     the soul,
        the sheathed assassin

the mind behind the brains
manipulates and wields
– her translations of desire
   cloaked in the feeblest of loyalties
   to the emptiest of symbols

though dazzled
as she sometimes is

        by the mounted
        swaggering illiterate
                       whose unexpected leaps

                       defy all precedence,
        trample all logic and intention,
        and flank, incredibly

the
slow
push
toward

clarity.

He'll play a swift, incisive match
and snake-quick to observe a flaw
in half a dozen moves dispatch
his victim. He'd rather lose than draw.

Has trouble playing by lamplight
for shadows still obscure his mind
but in the day his black or white
will dazzle his opponents blind;

yet makes mistakes, as one expects,
with moves the chess mole might descry,
but when the game will grow complex
revenges his simplicity.

He has no joy in turtle-chess,
dislikes the endgame, will turn green
with boredom, but see him press
with vicious bishop and killer queen;

for black or white, but never grey,
his chess spunk will intimidate
the circumspect. To watch him play
who would guess he's only eight?

Alonissos, Greece

A poor start is my prerequisite.
True, there are occasions I survive
a good beginning, or not knowing it
play a game I don't derive
from other games, make moves I don't repent,
and win sometimes by plan, not accident;

but on the whole a bad beginning,
an early, inextricable mess,
a quick disaster, seems to be the thing
that promises promising chess.
Cornered, minus a precocious queen,
quixotic knight nowhere to be seen,

or embarrassment of double-check
before I've slid a single bishop out,
the chess noose tightening round my neck,
effeminate pawns in total rout
and all come down to immediate grief –
with eagerness or something like relief

I recognize the place, feel at home,
search for some resource, move king or pawn;
a catatonic rook begins to roam
about the board, or bishops dawn
upon familiar darkness, accustomed strife.
My once-benighted game comes back to life.

An advantage based on pawn position
is a thing of relative permanence;
such are the infinitesimal, million,
petty contacts in parlors and kitchens,
daily arguments but without offence,
that consolidate the loved relation;

but based on the structure of the pieces,
since the pieces move from place to place,
relatively vain and ostentatious,
fickle, deceptive, gone without a trace –
the obsession with intellect or face,
the great encounters, the intensities.

How should she mind if Ferdinand had played
her false, not that being a king's son
entailed privileges, or that
being blessed by nature brought exemption

from the quibble of injustice? Whatever
Ferdinand might do was fair play
by blond Miranda, though soon enough
he'd exercise his deft obliquities,

sift, dissect, dispose of obstacles,
sacrifice his friends – as in every
royal calculation, not for his
advancement, but the general good.

The right wife for a young ambitious prince
who, likable as yet, plies his subtle
affectation of the casual
and an aptitude for small deceptions.

And though for a score of kingdoms
he should wrangle, she'll bring him benefit
of love's immunities, confessing him
a dangerous and sentimental man,

and go on loving him despite
the nimble move-manipulator
engaged in Neapolitan intrigue,
his talk of strategy, his abstracted look.

'considered the greatest German player since Lasker'
– Chess Dictionary.

Old Hübner, judging me a dunce,
kindly offered to play me once;
made a few perfunctory moves
with cool indifference, as behooves
a master matched against a fool
who can't distinguish chess from pool.
The game went on, I pushed my wood,
then Hübner coughed and said, "Quite good."
I checked his king, he said, "What next?",
and even looked a trifle vexed
that I should trouble his repose
obliging him to interpose
a knight, a bishop or a rook,
which I swept in and nimbly took
so that he now began to think
and forge a pawn chain link by link,
which I unlocked by subtle ploys –
he fidgeted and made a noise;
with puckered brow and nervous smile
he opened an attacking file
but weakened an important square;
with mixed sobriety and flair
I posted a commanding knight
and doubled rooks. His men in flight,
his king encastled in a sieve,

deprived of all initiative,
old Hübner tugged his bearded jaw
and offered me a timely draw,
to which from kindness I agreed
since even masters, pricked, will bleed.

mundus alter et idem

"Those are my best days when I shake with fear,"
was your opening move.
To which I counter-quoted
the dark night of the soul
or ignorant armies on a checkered field,
taking comfort in your presence
across the rosewood that aligned us.
And so the game proceeded.
"Light marbles into dark,
you'd think it should be otherwise."
"Night reconciles me to day,
black gives me an advantage."
"O Lucifer in starlight."
"O unalterable law of a sunny disposition."
"You are the better player."
"And you, the better poet."
"We are all amateurs,
blundering our loves like unaccomplished royals."
"Yes, and chess reminds us of our incompetence
in any true thing we might wish to do."
"Like the daimon of black
jetted by extinguishings."
"Like crown or diamond cabala
imagining the majesty of snow."
"With this move," you said,
bright day is done."

"And we are for the dark," I capped
your apt allusion,
giving the game away –
the game of balancing black and white
in mirrored combinations of imperial tact
to the twilight of the endgame
and the chronicled draw,
matching phrase for phrase,
trading pawn for pawn,
allowing no difference between us.

The fiscal bishops tear their mitred hair,
in tortured resignation come upon
another botched account they cannot square.
The kingdom's in the hands of Shylock Pawn.

The king has squandered all his revenues
and brought his mandate into mere disgrace,
suspecting there is always more to lose:
his queen, the game, self-possession, hope, face.

And so the king refuses to lament
what his exchequer cannot solve or mend
but spends again what is already spent.
It is as if he doubted at the end

prosperity could balance or redress
the regal magnanimity of loss.

And in this case it is so, not because the person to whom we give
the explanation already knows rules, but because in another sense
he is already master of a game. – Philosophical Investigations, 31

1. The rules by which we play
   are only the conditions
   of the game we happen to be playing.

2. They are not laws or immutable decrees
   but necessary accidents,
   evolutionary afterthoughts,
   bones that tenon our parquetry.

3. The king, for example,
   campaigning in the Orkneys
   of his extravagance,
   boasting of coastal sway and scope,
   is the only piece that can be checked.

4. This was not given in Plato's handbook
   of the eternal Form of chess
   spelled out in *topos ouranios*
   but happened somewhere along the way,
   say, between India and Cambridge.

5. We are apprentices of the ludicrous.
   The game precedes the rules
   as we feint and thrust
   along the lines
   of a prior immeasurable quadratic
   determining the set of our precisions,
   specialists of the general.

6. Thus I decide to play
   scholarly and frivolous as Hamlet
   consulting the Tarot
   on a Sunday afternoon
   over tea and scones
   in my rooms above the Quad;
   or, as it may be, to speculate
   on Manichaean doubles
   in the locus of illusion,
   the kingdom of warring particulars
   squared in celluloid;
   or to set an army of thoughts
   marching down the page
   towards ruin and imperial concessions.

7. But now I move this pawn
   to block your clever theoretical bishop
   and lock him into innocuous stasis
   as the current of intrigue moves elsewhere
   across the board that frames
   our choices and encounters.

8. As for the rules, let us say
   they consecrate
   the freedom of the pieces
   as they do our Seleucid flourishes
   in the intricate roil of desire,
   the first tactical gestures,
   risk and probe of language
   crowned by the syntax of consummation
   as it happens to develop
   between late afternoon and dusk.

9. And this is like chess
   and not like chess,
   and chess is also not like chess
   but like that other game
   whose borders defy the surveyor
   in the realm where the rules merely ransom
   our dark affinities and compulsions.

Praying for an edge
only water may give
and God's inviolable stone,
I receive my instrument.

Whetted and honed,
the blade is in love with the wood.
It scores these lines
in the plane of the board

with an ardor and skill
I cannot match
to guide my pilgrimage
toward the arbor of perfections.

Knowing it a sacrament,
what else can I do
but trim the words
and whittle each thought

and carve the emblems
of this brittle world
awry
as the chess king's tilted cross?

translated from the Greek of Andreas Karavis

1

Reluctant to surrender
a single pawn, he moves with
scrupulous exactitude,
with calculated power
in agile bishop or path-
clearing knight, bestows the hood

of the executioner
on his implacable queen,
giving you nothing for free.
The makings of a master
there, could he but determine
to take chess seriously –

serious in the progress
of the game, but afterwards
suspecting the distortion
of the mind seduced by chess,
keeps his sense of proportion
and will not dream of chessboards.

2

Reads the board like a blueprint;
develops a certain theme;
looks for patterns in the jell
of integers; will invent
an architectonic game,
intricate, symmetrical;

plans defence or attack
down to the decimal point,
in love with rigorous play.
Yet, he'll ply an early rook,
lose a knight as if he meant
to dispose of chess debris

or plead unorthodox chess,
giving chance a chance, to try
at the cost of victory
the pleasures of surprise, less
in love with rigorous play
than with possibility.

3

The αρχαι, the Grail, the *Ding*
an sich – to these he equates
the noetic tyranny
of chess; says winning's losing
since that but approximates
to the perfect victory

(what should be, what never was),
discrepancy increasing
by perpetual approach;
thus he pursues exchanges,
abhorring complication,
preferring little to much,

knowing that, how mind may range,
the result will disappoint
the born idealist who
sees that chess is life's revenge
for the dream best left undreamt
and the gift of mastery.

4

His game's not in winning – not
in not winning, either –
but in daring gravity:
pawns begin to levitate
over each pragmatic square
on a meditative spree

and the pieces jump about
like ecstatic astronauts
playing tag in hyperspace.
Chess: a poet's antidote
to daily *don'ts*, nightly *nots*,
and the recommended grace

of accomplishing the valid.
My friend would call it moon chess
or a kind of lunar zen
as he empties out his head
to construct his masterpiece
and surrender all his men.

Spontaneous in his moves,
with an air of disregard,
the reckless development
of the game is what he loves;
flicks the pieces off the board
good-naturedly impatient

of those who deliberate
their moves. Smiles and flicking wrists
may have, in chess, their terrors.
Here, then, is the chess coquette,
tactician, whose game consists
in clock-extorting errors

from too impressionable
or leisurely opponents.
Odd how, though unambitious,
half his pawns are queenable
in minutes, whose game exploits
the accidents of blitz-chess.

Playing her, I wonder: can a
harmless two year old named Hannah
spring a trap to ambush my advantage.
She remembers all the pieces
quite as if by anamnesis
but moves them like a Tartar on the rampage.

She'll cram two pieces on one square
for company; to my despair
with her sharp elbow she'll unhorse my knight;
and if I patiently explain
it can't be done, she'll end the reign
of my poor royal couple with one bite!

Here's her chubby rook who'll dish up
splinter-fare; her skinny bishop
sneaks out darkly on a secret mission;
there's her knight astride his bronco
trampling hard upon a pawn co-
llaborating with the opposition.

She knocks my queen upon her face,
pries the felt from my king's base,
and does not need ability or luck.
For she by child-right will win
while I must lose through discipline
that cannot match her innocence and pluck.

So, returned from the wars,
few trophies, many scars;
have made obeisance
to my phlegmatic prince
and shuffled from the hall
blessed by the cardinal.
(The queen was rather brief,
gave me her handkerchief.)
The great lords risked little,
kept their tents in battle,
kept their heads to the last
and filled the treasure chest.
Nor have I love to spare
for all these cavaliers:
some went for adventure,
and others, I am sure,
because they loved to kill,
some to display their skill
at graceful caracole
or dye a lady's shawl
in rich Saracen blood.
The common soldiers shed
some cold retreating sweat
but now have little doubt
of valour in the field.
I swear at times I'm filled
with treasure of contempt
to think that I have camped

with cowards, parasites,
shirkers, lordlings, prelates
and all that scurvy brood.
Just wait. The next crusade
I'll hear a different drum,
enter Jerusalem –
but as a captive knight
and loyal proselyte.

The moon queen spreads her shadow across the board and leers triumphantly, little dracules of plutonium circulating in her blood. I shift uneasily and hope this is just another hereditary episode as I watch her pi and bolix the pieces which miraculously sprout glass prunts and rose bracts. They are inlaid with shagreen and amboyna wood and flaunt a spurious elegance as if in compensation for some pedestrian infirmity which I obscurely share. I know I am in serious trouble but can find no way to devil up my game which remains in the last throes of immedicable woe. I want a level playing field and drag my bilboquet across the slope, rubbing out the grout lines while I clear away the opposition, but the pieces rise again from a steep terracotta floor to haunt my illegible notations. I need to put more rhumba in my moves but am paralyzed by the moon queen's lemurine enormities. I switch to another mode and begin to play swagger chess but she anticipates the maneuver with a clowder of pawns armed with hunger claws. Tangled in a bat of lathes and struts, I realize I am in zugzwang and prepare to tip my king, but discover I am not even permitted to lose. I rummage among boxes of books and crates of cassettes for some nimble defense that will enable me to abandon the game entirely. The moon queen remains unmoved. Suddenly, I am limping from square to square as the board expands to the horizon.

THE PIN

Chess is particularly the game of the unappreciated. – Richard Reti

1   (Antagonists)

He was perfectly appeased;
from the start, elected.
She called him her dark prince;

but the paradox was always there,
the intrinsic contradiction
of a conqueror who couldn't ride.

She was fond of horses,
their glorious flanks, the small
earthquakes of their galloping;

it was uninstructed power
she loved, and ignorant beauty;
she loved the knight for his horse.

The Greek actor who played
a raving Agamemnon
she could never forget; he strode

upon the stage in buskins,
oncus and mask, but she was stricken
by the muscles of his calves.

Sex came hard for her; she grappled
with the duty of its pleasure,
as a presbyterian queen

despises what she craves, in whom
the animal of desire
is confined. She loved horses

and beautiful actors, the backs
of laborers, dishevelled men
in parks, but the marriage bed

was her calamity. She called him
her dark prince. She quivered
like Gwynevere. She moaned like Isolde.

She awaited the issue of his
pilgrimage, chaste as Penelope,
yet dreamed her nightly elopements.

2   (Antagonists)

A conqueror who couldn't ride
hankering for Persepolis,
he praised the beauty of the mind;

though appreciating, too,
the beauty of the flesh, tried
to compensate by exercise

of intellect the feared
deficiency of his lesser self.
Thus he carried on and rode

as best he could, a crippled
centaur, who might at times even
appear invincible.

The need for chess supremacy
(of sorts) determined the calibre
of his chosen opposition

(though himself debarred from choice
except when previously chosen);
the need for deference, a brazen

panoply, a fancy moniker,
governed his kinesis. He loved
ideas by equestrian

default, managing his wooden
steed with a certain svelte
ineptitude, prodigious suitor,

white knight, dark prince, presumptive king,
whose rambles round the board were those
of some bridal peregrine.

3   (The Game)

When he bent to kiss her, after
one of their disputes, she flinched:
"You remind me of you," she said.

Nature, she thought, was fixed;
the bishop's slant must always be
diagonal; the knight

cranky and elliptic; the rook
an elegant bruiser, and
so on, *usque ad finem*.

Human chess, he said, was flexible –
the board, perhaps, eternal,
but the moves, to some extent,

a matter of mere choice:
the queen mounted on a palfrey,
the bishops honest, and the knights

demoted to the infantry.
She would reply: "The game you play
is fixed and recognizable,

the sequence of your moves
an absolute revelation."
No doubt she would be right

in their metaphysical dispute.
But then he might decide to lose.
But then he might decide to stay

with his appropriate game –
necessity an act of choice –
despite the foreseeable mate.

4   (Excursus)

Metaphysics, much like chess,
is a game of counter-moves;
and both resemble marriage

in the complication of the
argument, tactics superseding
tact. It is an imperishable

antinomy to which
we must devote a new critique
of pure dissimulation.

White, black; substance, accident;
man, woman; summed up in the endless
marriage of conflicting minds.

Set or malleable? At what point
does freedom break the circle?
If only Spinoza had married

or played the Morphy of his age
he might have clobbered Leibniz
and gained accreditation

as metaphysical referee,
judge of nuptial duplicities,
I might apply to for a verdict.

5   (The Sequel)

He came into a vision of himself
he most had coveted,
delivered from self-oblivion,

the perpetual suspicion
of personal insignificance.
He strode up and down the balcony

knowing he was watched by her.
Life became theatre, and she,
both audience and leading lady,

noted how he lit his cigarette
with a Belmondo flourish,
reading the smoke for oracles.

He spoke about the past, as if
no one else had ever had one,
to exorcise a mother's ghost

or abuse an equestrian wife,
while she regarded his performance,
amused, interested and horrified.

But truly when he met her
it was like being recognized
at the airport, charter ticket

magically transformed
into a first-class pass,
courtesy of the airline;

or like a master at Reykjavik
observing his every move
posted up in majuscule.

Who could compete with such
a metamorphosis? Everywhere
he went he heard the cameras

whirring and clicking, each pose
recorded for posterity,
each word preserved in amber.

How could he fail to respond,
being once again elect, rescued
from primeval limitation?

One leans into the mirror and speaks:
  "I wish to remain my elemental self,
    whether mezzanine villain playing
      nasty canasta, or hunkering
        on the board in the slumber of the innocent –

neither either nor neither
  but only this material presence
    carved from hardwood, cambered
      and inwedged, dreaming in Sumerian
        the tiny grandeur of my unlikelihood."

Yet every piece, stripped of particular shape,
  dies an identical neural death,
    disappearing so thoroughly
      not even the pressure on the hand remains
        as wood's lightest reminiscence.

Gone the rook lacquered and squat,
  the bishop's slim nacelle,
    the king's tall elegance and queen's trim cut,
      the knight rampant and hot
        among a splintering of pawns.

They disappear so thoroughly
　nothing remains of billet and chip
　　or the brute weight of an army's lumber.
　　　Only abstract black and spectral white
　　　　hovering in airs of shadow and light.

ACKNOWLEDGMENTS

Some of these poems have appeared in *The Antigonish Review*,
The Atlantic Monthly, *Canadian Literature*, *The Formalist*, *Index*,
The Malahat Review, *Matrix*, *Parnassus*, and *The Sewanee Review*.